daylig

Bible S

M000095524

A DVD-based study series
Study Guide

ROMANS

The Letter That Changed The World

With Mart De Haan & Jimmy DeYoung

A DVD-based study series
Study Guide

ROMANS

The Letter That Changed The World
With Mart De Haan & Jimmy DeYoung

Twelve Lessons for Group Exploration

DISCOVERY HOUSE

P U B L I S H E R S®

The DayLight Bible Studies are based on programs produced by
Day of Discovery, **a Bible-teaching TV series of RBC Ministries.**

© 2010 by Discovery House Publishers

Discovery House Publishers is affiliated with RBC Ministries,
Grand Rapids, Michigan.

Requests for permission to quote from this book should be directed to:
Permissions Department
Discovery House Publishers
P.O. Box 3566
Grand Rapids, MI 49501
or contact us by email at permissionsdept@dhp.org

Study questions by Andrew Sloan
Interior design by Sherri L. Hoffman
Cover design by Jeremy Culp
Cover image from istockphoto.com

ISBN: 978-1-57293-391-0

Printed in the United States of America

Third printing 2012

CONTENTS

Mail Call

Down through the annals of mankind, great men and women have used the vehicle of the personal or public letter to convey great truths and to express valuable ideas. Many of these letters have taken on historical significance that has extended far beyond the era in which the words were penned.

In 49 BC, Caesar wrote a letter to Cicero in which he warned the emperor of the importance of avoiding civil strife.

In the 1500s, Martin Luther penned notes to his friends in which he defended his beliefs and denied the accusations that he was a religious heretic.

In the early 1600s, the great Galileo sent a letter to fellow astronomer Kepler in which he waxed eloquently about the magnificent heavenly bodies he had observed through his improved telescope.

In the 1960s, Martin Luther King took up paper while in a Birmingham, Alabama, jail to explain in a letter why he felt the civil rights movement had to proceed, penning his superb statement: "injustice anywhere is a threat to justice everywhere."

None of these letters, though, no matter how significant they were to their era, can carry the weight of a document scratched on parchment during the first century AD—a document that was either penned by or dictated by a Jewish convert to Christianity named Paul. This letter, which was directed to Christians who lived in the capital city of Rome, Italy, contained teachings and doctrines that would change the world.

Paul's letter was a shot across the bow in a society in which the ruler was supreme and in which the individual person had little value. It was a surprising document in a world where there had always been a clear line of demarcation between Jews and Gentiles. This letter was countercultural and revolutionary in a day when Rome ruled its citizens—both in Italy and throughout the Empire—with an iron fist.

Bible teachers Mart De Haan, Jimmy DeYoung, along with some experts in both Roman culture and biblical research, have teamed up to give us a refreshing and intriguing picture of Paul's letter and how it was received in its day. Each study presents another new perspective on Paul's words—how they would have been accepted in his day and how they still are to be applied today in our lives.

So jump on as we take a tour of the places in Israel that reflect first-century Roman culture and the places in Rome itself that help us get a glimpse of what it must have been like to receive a letter like this one soon after it had been penned by the great apostle.

History, theology, and biblical background combine in *Romans: The Letter that Changed The World* to bring us new insights into one of the most fascinating letters ever written.

—Dave Branon
Editor

Rome's Fundamental Flaw

DAYLIGHT PREVIEW

The Roman Connection

Why does a book that was written to advance the message of a faith centered in Israel focus so much on a country so far away? Why did Paul concern himself to such a great degree with Rome and how Rome affected the Christians in Italy, the Christians in Israel at the time, and all of Christianity? Mart De Haan and Jimmy DeYoung begin to answer those questions with a visit to the site of an archaeological dig that reveals much about the connection of Roman culture, Jewish culture, and Christianity. Join them as they walk the streets of Scythopolis, one of the cities of the Decapolis during the great Roman Empire.

——— COME TOGETHER ———

Icebreaker Questions

1. Do you enjoy learning about faraway places? If so, how do you go about doing so?

2. Have you ever been to Rome? Have you ever been to one of the Roman replica cities, such as Beth Shean in Israel?

3. What is the closest you have been to an earthquake?

FINDING DAYLIGHT

Experience the Video

Feel free to jot down notes as you watch the presentation by Jimmy DeYoung and Mart De Haan. Use the space below for those notes.

────────────────── VIDEO NOTES ──────────────────

Beth Shean (Scythopolis)

The glory of the Roman Empire

A fundamental flaw and a letter from Paul

Destruction of Beth Shean

Christianity vs. Paganism

Temples in Rome: Pantheon

Roman gods and Paul

Cult of the Caesars

Mart's questions about Romans

WALKING IN THE DAYLIGHT

Discussion Time

——————————— UNDERSTAND THE CULTURE ———————————
Background Questions

1. Why do you think it was so important to Roman colonists to build replicas of Rome?

2. The Roman belief and value system included a pluralism of gods and a low level of morality. How does that fundamental flaw of the Roman Empire compare to what's going on in the world today?

3. Although emperor worship doesn't occur today, how is personality, celebrity, or hero worship still relevant? How do you find yourself sucked into that pattern?

Discussion/Application Questions

1. **In Romans 1:1-7, Paul introduces his letter to the Romans with some important information.**

    a. How did Paul view Jesus Christ?

    b. How did Paul view himself?

2. **The letter to the Romans is one of the few letters Paul wrote to a church he had not planted and had never even visited. But finally, as Paul notes in Romans 15:23-29, he anticipates that after a brief stop in Jerusalem he's finally going to be able to go to Rome and visit the people there. Read Romans 1:8-15.**

    a. How did Paul feel about visiting the believers in Rome?

    b. What effect do you suppose the fact that those believers lived in the imperial capital had on Paul's feelings?

3. **The letter to the Romans will clearly explain the gospel, which Paul characterizes in Romans 1:16-17.**

    a. How did Paul summarize the gospel here?

b.   Would there be intensified reasons to be "ashamed of the gospel" in the capital city of the Roman Empire?

Reflecting on your own life: How does our culture sometimes make us seem to be "ashamed of the gospel"?

4. **Paul makes some astounding claims in Romans 1:18-20.**

    a.   What does nature teach us about spiritual realities?

    b.   What does Paul mean when he says that people are "without excuse"?

5. **We usually read Romans 1:21-32 thinking of our time—our culture. Read it with your new understanding of the world into which Paul was taking this message.**

    a.   How do you suppose this message was received in the pagan Roman world with its pantheon of gods?

    b.   How was the gospel a threat to Rome?

Reflecting on today's culture: How is the gospel a threat to the world today?

6. **Mart De Haan reflects on why Paul would express such concern about the kind of worship and spirituality he had seen across the empire. The danger, according to Paul, is that our Creator cares enough to be angry when He sees those He loves being ruined by gods that are not God and by worship that is worthless.**

   Reflecting on your own life: How is that expression of alarm or concern a wake-up call to you?

DAYLIGHT ON PRAYER

A Time to Share

1. Paul wrote to the believers in Rome, "I am not ashamed of the gospel, because it is the power of God for the salvation of everyone who believes" (Romans 1:16). In what area of your life do you sense a need to ask God for more of His power?

2. Do you have a prayer request to share with the group?

DAYLIGHT AHEAD

In our next session, Mart De Haan and Jimmy DeYoung stay in Beth Shean, where they help us understand the architecture and use of a first-century theater. In so doing, they also shed light on one of Paul's reasons for penning his important letter to the Romans.

A People Problem

DAYLIGHT PREVIEW

A Lesson at the Theater

One of the central features of the mini-Romes that were built all over the Roman Empire was the theater. In this lesson, Mart and Jimmy visit the ruins of a 7,000-seat theater in Beth Shean, one of the ten cities of the Decapolis built on both sides of the Jordan. Using this site as a backdrop, Jimmy and Mart teach a valuable lesson about one of Paul's key teachings as found in *Romans: The Letter that Changed the World.*

--- COME TOGETHER ---

Icebreaker Questions

1. When are you most prone to overeating: Parties? Holiday dinners? All-you-can-eat restaurants?

2. What's the biggest crowd you can remember being in at a concert or stage production?

3. What's the best seat you've ever had at a concert, play, or sporting event? What's the worst seat?

FINDING DAYLIGHT

Experience the Video

Feel free to jot down notes as you watch the presentation by Jimmy DeYoung and Mart De Haan. Use the space below for those notes.

────────────── **VIDEO NOTES** ──────────────

The theater

Two audiences of the apostle Paul

"Leveling the playing field"

The faultline of sin

Mart and Jimmy's wrap-up

WALKING IN THE DAYLIGHT

Discussion Time

UNDERSTAND THE CULTURE
Background Questions

1. According to Jimmy DeYoung, the practice in the Roman Empire was for people to gorge themselves with food, go out to a vomitorium to relieve themselves, and then eat more. How is indulgence expressed in the world today?

2. In his letter to the Romans, Paul is dealing with a people problem. The church brought together Jews and Gentiles in a new and unprecedented way. However, using the symbol of a theater, the Jews had enjoyed the best seats in the house—making them reluctant to regard Gentile believers with an equal status. What dynamics might cause a separation between first-class and second-class citizens in the church today?

DISCOVER GOD'S WORD
Discussion/Application Questions

1. **As we saw in the last session, Romans 1:18-32 focuses on Gentiles. In 2:17-29 Paul speaks specifically to Jews.**

   a. According to this passage, what advantages did the Jews feel they had over the Gentiles?

b. What did Paul say was the reality in regard to these perceived advantages? How does he describe a true Jew?

2. **Dr. Douglas Moo points out that Paul says, in essence, "The Gentiles are involved in idolatry; they're rejecting the true God of the Bible and making their own gods. But you Jews have done basically the same thing. You've made Torah [the first five books of the Old Testament] your law, something so important that you've put *it* in place of God."**

    a. Is there a danger of people in the church doing something like that today?

    Reflecting on your own life: To what extent can you identify with that danger?

3. **Using a string of Old Testament quotations in Romans 3:9-20, Paul concludes his analysis of the state of both Jews and Gentiles.**

    How does Paul's message level the playing field between Jews and Gentiles? Between any two groups today?

4. **As Dr. Moo points out, rather than beginning the book of Romans by talking about the gospel, Paul begins by talking about why the**

good news is needed. So at the end of chapter 3, beginning in 3:21, Paul begins describing the good news. Read Romans 3:21-26.

a. How do we acquire the righteousness we need?

b. What does it mean for a person to have "faith in [Christ's] blood" (v. 25)?

5. Mart De Haan observes, "We're all inclined to give ourselves the consideration and honor that God alone deserves. None of us can sacrifice enough, worship enough, or work enough to remove God's judgment from us. We are asked instead to trust in God's own provision of a sacrifice: the offering of His one and only Son."

Reflecting on your own life: How do you know that this is where your trust lies?

DAYLIGHT ON PRAYER

A Time to Share

1. How have you experienced the power of the gospel to level the playing field between people? Do you see a need for more of that in your relationships with fellow believers? How can you pray for that to be more prevalent in your life—your church?

2. Spend some time praying for concerns in your own life as well as burdens you have for others.

 DAYLIGHT AHEAD

Moving on from Beth Shean, Jimmy DeYoung and Mart De Haan venture north and west to Caesarea, a city built by Rome on the shore of the Mediterranean Sea. Here they will visit a great outdoor amphitheater as they examine Rome's treatment of its citizens. We'll find out that despite Rome's best efforts, the leaders of the empire failed to give the people what they needed most.

Pax Romana

DAYLIGHT PREVIEW

What Rome Couldn't Provide

The seashore city of Caesarea is a good example of how the Roman government cared for its people. Typical of the cities built by the great Roman Empire, it had theaters and other places of entertainment so the people of the empire could have the same kinds of choices offered the ones who lived in Italy. Herod and other leaders gave the people a time of peace and plenty—complete with entertainment, food, and comfort. But despite the "religious" edifices of Rome, the government could not provide the most essential element. And that is one reason Paul wrote the book of Romans—to explain what that essential element is.

COME TOGETHER

Icebreaker Questions

1. Have you ever searched for or collected seashells?

2. Do you have childhood memories of going to the circus?

3. How close to April 15 do you usually finish your income tax return?

FINDING DAYLIGHT

Experience the Video

Feel free to jot down notes as you watch the presentation by Jimmy DeYoung and Mart De Haan. Use the space below for those notes.

——————————— **VIDEO NOTES** ———————————

Caesarea

Herod

Herod and biblical connections

The theater and Roman entertainment

Rome's Coliseum

Rome's complete care for its people

Pax Romana—a spiritual vacuum

Romans and the good news

Paul's counterculture teaching

WALKING IN THE DAYLIGHT

Discussion Time

—————— UNDERSTAND THE CULTURE ——————
Background Question

We learn in this session that the coliseum in Rome, and venues like it throughout the empire, were used as a safety valve for public aggressiveness—i.e., that through these events people could somehow get rid of their anger and dissatisfaction. Do you see any parallels to that situation today?

Discussion/Application Questions

1. **In this session we discover a strong relationship between the Caesars in Rome and the land of Israel in the times of the New Testament. Read Luke 2:1-7.**

    a. What evidence do we see of that strong relationship in this passage?

    b. What part did Caesar Augustus play in fulfilling the Old Testament prophecy of Micah 5:2 that the Messiah would be born in Bethlehem?

2. **In Matthew 2:1-6 we are introduced to Herod the Great, who, though not a Jew, was appointed by the Romans as a client king over Judea.**

    Why was Herod "disturbed," or "troubled," by the words of the Magi?

3. **Matthew 2:7-16 continues the story of Jesus' birth in relation to Herod and the Magi.**

    What does Mart De Haan mean when he says, "The conflict between Herod and Jesus was only a foreshadowing of the conflict between imperial Rome and the followers of the resurrected Christ"?

4. In Romans 5:1-8 Paul mentions the peace that believers have in Christ. Mart De Haan states, "By the time it reached its zenith, the Roman Empire was providing unprecedented social and material services to its citizens. But instead of producing satisfaction, its bread, circuses, and enforced peace—its *Pax Romana*—left a spiritual vacuum that its gods could not fill. Then, 'at just the right time' (Romans 5:6), a message of hope—of true provision—was heard in the theater of despair."

How did Christ provide that message of hope and true peace?

5. Dr. Paul Maier states that the centerpiece of Paul's letter to Rome is passages like this one in chapter 5, where the apostle talks about how we get right with God—and the answer is that God gets right with *us*!

a. What does that mean?

b. Why would this concept seem very strange to pagans, since the whole idea in Greco-Roman religion was to work for your salvation?

c. How is that concept countercultural in our world today?

DAYLIGHT ON PRAYER

A Time to Share

1. In what area of your life do you have the most peace? In what area do you have the least peace?

2. What prayer concerns would you like to share with the group?

3. Close by praying for those concerns and by asking God to give each person His peace.

DAYLIGHT AHEAD

What do you have to do to be saved? Walk stairs? Go to a temple? The Romans had their ideas about this—but Paul had a very different concept. While visiting the port city of Caesarea and while telling the story of a Roman soldier and a Christian apostle, Jimmy DeYoung and Mart De Haan explain the only true way a person can experience the good news.

Faith Alone

DAYLIGHT PREVIEW

The Story of a Soldier

It was through the story of a Roman soldier—a centurion, in fact—that Paul was able to clarify his most important message of his book: Salvation by faith alone. For many Roman people and for far too many people down through the ages, getting to God has proved far more complicated than it needs to be. Jimmy DeYoung and Mart De Haan point this out as they share something that happened to the apostle Peter and the centurion. You'll see salvation at work—and you'll understand why Mart calls the gospel "A Divine Sea of Love."

COME TOGETHER

Icebreaker Questions

1. Do you enjoy learning about history? If so, how do you do that?

2. What is the most memorable set of stairs you can remember climbing?

3. How vividly do you remember your dreams? Any worth mentioning?

FINDING DAYLIGHT

Experience the Video

Feel free to jot down notes as you watch the presentation by Jimmy DeYoung and Mart De Haan. Use the space below for those notes.

—————————————— **VIDEO NOTES** ——————————————

Temples in Rome

Working to please God

The Holy Stairs

A message of faith alone

Peter and the centurion

A turning point

What Cornelius heard

Romans, cults, and the good news

God's extra provision

"A Divine Sea of Love"

WALKING IN THE DAYLIGHT

Discussion Time

UNDERSTAND THE CULTURE

Background Questions

1. How did you feel as you watched people climbing the Scala Sancta in Rome—the stairs that, according to tradition, led to where Pontius Pilate met with Jesus? (The stairs were supposedly taken from Jerusalem to Rome in the fourth century.)

2. How do people today, even within the church, still try to "climb to their eternal reward" by their own efforts? To what extent is that an issue in your own life?

———— DISCOVER GOD'S WORD ————

Discussion/Application Questions

1. **The book of Acts records a pivotal story about the apostle Peter and a Roman army officer stationed at Caesarea, the headquarters for the Roman forces occupying Palestine. Begin the story by reading Acts 10:1-8.**

    What kind of a person was Cornelius?

2. **As we see in Acts 10:9-20, Cornelius wasn't the only person God was speaking to.**

    Why did Peter recoil at this vision?

3. **Going with the men sent by Cornelius, Peter traveled about thirty miles north of Joppa, where he was staying, to Caesarea. Cornelius was expecting him and had invited his relatives and close friends to come to his house. Acts 10:34-35 records Peter's first words to this large gathering of people.**

    What do these words addressed to Cornelius and the other Gentiles gathered at his house show about Peter's change of heart?

4. **In Acts 10:36-43 Peter told the group about the good news of Jesus.**

Although Cornelius tried to please God and live a good life, what did he still need?

5. **Read Acts 10:44-48 to see what happened next.**

Why would the response of these people be a turning point in the history of the New Testament?

6. **Mart De Haan points out that Cornelius was one of the first examples of a person who experienced, as a non-Jewish person, the truth of the message of probably the most important letter of the New Testament—Paul's letter to the Romans. Read Romans 5:6-8.**

How does Paul's letter to the Romans, in passages like this, reinforce the importance of Peter's message as well as the response of his listeners?

7. **Mart De Haan goes on to say, "Walking among Roman ruins here in Israel seems like such a tangible connection to the people and events of the New Testament. When Jesus was here, Caesar was law, Caesar was the power. Caesar held administrative control over this occupied land. Eventually Roman soldiers even executed Jesus in a most demeaning and agonizing manner—by crucifixion. But now, some two thousand years later, the Roman Empire is but a memory revived by shattered columns, broken idols, pottery shards washed by the Mediterranean here in Caesarea. Rome is dead, but Jesus is**

alive. And in the end, it's not human power and effort to swim to God, but a 'divine sea of love' that reaches to us."

Reflecting on your own life: How are you personally experiencing the reality that "Jesus is alive"?

DAYLIGHT ON PRAYER

A Time to Share

1. How has God's "divine sea of love" touched your life?

2. How could you position yourself to be swept over by that sea of love in a fresh way?

3. What prayer requests would you like to share with the group?

DAYLIGHT AHEAD

Ever find yourself in what appears to be the wrong place at the wrong time? That's what seems to happen to Mart De Haan and Jimmy DeYoung in our next session as they visit a reenactment of drills by Roman soldiers—only to discover that they are far too close to the action. Join Mart and Jimmy as they teach us about the stoic virtues of the Roman Empire, as they point out the one important thing the Romans were missing—and as they dodge the swords!

Rome: The Good and the Bad

DAYLIGHT PREVIEW

A Day at the Hippodrome

One of the buildings the Romans built in each of their mini-Romes scattered throughout the empire was the hippodrome—a place for horse races and other athletic games. In the city of Jerash, Jimmy DeYoung and Mart De Haan stopped by for a live demonstration of how gladiators in the days of the Roman Empire battled each other. This activity was symbolic of the way Rome kept its people under subjection—with power and the threat of death.

COME TOGETHER

Icebreaker Questions

1. Do you consider yourself a disciplined person? What is one example of that?

2. What kind of make-believe games did you play as a child? Did you ever "reenact" things?

3. How difficult is it to watch theatrical presentations of the gladiatorial events in Rome?

FINDING DAYLIGHT

Experience the Video

Feel free to jot down notes as you watch the presentation by Jimmy DeYoung and Mart De Haan. Use the space below for those notes.

────────────── **VIDEO NOTES** ──────────────

Jerash

Circus Maximus; hippodrome

Roman law code

Stoic virtues

Romans and spirituality

Paul's letter

WALKING IN THE DAYLIGHT

Discussion Time

————————— UNDERSTAND THE CULTURE —————————
Background Questions

1. We see that the Roman law code was greatly respected and has had tremendous subsequent influence on the world's law codes—plus Roman society was also known by a long list of virtues. On the other hand, we see the reality of gladiatorial combat, in which it was okay to kill somebody if it was done within the realm of "entertainment," a public game of some kind.

    a. How do you suppose the Romans got around those seeming inconsistencies?

    b. Do you see similar inconsistencies in our own culture?

2. Some of the Roman virtues mentioned in the DVD are discipline, faithfulness to the law, respect for authority, tenacity, industriousness, and dutifulness.

    a. How would these virtues contribute to the success and expansion of the empire?

    b. What was still missing or incomplete?

Discussion/Application Questions

1. Reflecting on the reenactment that Mart De Haan and Jimmy DeYoung experienced at Jerash, Mart said, "Jimmy and I could see that by discipline and hard work Roman soldiers and citizens could know that they were in good standing with their Caesar. But spiritually, the Romans really had no idea if they were measuring up to the requirements of their gods. Although Rome had brought peace to the empire, the people had no source of personal peace in this life nor hope for the life to come. They had no way of knowing whether their lives would be given a thumbs up or a thumb of death."

   In Romans 5:12-14 Paul discusses the origin of the sentence of death that is upon every human being.

   a. What was the effect of Adam's sin?

   b. What does Paul mean that Adam "was a pattern of the one to come" (v. 14)?

2. **In Romans 5:15-19 Paul counters the bad news with the good news.**

   How would you compare and contrast the trespass of the first man with the gift of the second man?

3. **Paul summarizes the bad news and the good news in Romans 6:23.**

   What does this mean in the gladiatorial terms of a thumbs up or a thumb of death?

4. **Mart De Haan notes that when the significance of Paul's message was understood it would challenge everything the Roman world believed about how people relate to one another and to the one true God.**

   Why is that just as true today as it was then?

DAYLIGHT ON PRAYER

A Time to Share

1. Romans 5:15-19 and 6:23 speak of God's gifts—by grace, of salvation, righteousness, and eternal life. What are the appropriate responses to these gifts?

2. Spend some time as a group thanking God for these marvelous gifts.

3. How can the group support you in prayer today?

DAYLIGHT AHEAD

Could the Romans learn to use the law as God designed it? That's a key question for them, because the law was extremely important to the Empire. In our next session, Jimmy DeYoung and Mart De Haan use a mirror and a reflecting pool to explain how God uses the law.

The Law as a Mirror

DAYLIGHT PREVIEW

What the Romans Missed

Paul had some bad news for the people in Romans—especially those who were attempting to live according to the Jewish law, the Torah. He wanted them to know that the law could not earn them God's approval. This would have been surprising to these people, because to the Romans the law was everything. Sure, there was value in the law—like a reflection in a pool of water it could reveal what the people looked like. But Paul wanted the people to know that the law could not fix the problems they might find.

—————— COME TOGETHER ——————

Icebreaker Questions

1. Jimmy still keeps and uses a mirror his daughter gave him, even though it has seen better days. Do you have something like that?

2. What's your favorite mirror in your home?

3. What memory do you have of a body of water that presented a clear or stunning reflection?

FINDING DAYLIGHT

Experience the Video

Feel free to jot down notes as you watch the presentation by Jimmy DeYoung and Mart De Haan. Use the space below for those notes.

——————————VIDEO NOTES ——————————

Paul's solution

Jews and the law

A mirror and the law

The struggle to be good

The human dilemma and Paul's good news

Mart's final word

WALKING IN THE DAYLIGHT

Discussion Time

DISCOVER GOD'S WORD

Discussion/Application Questions

1. Mart De Haan points out that the amazing solution Paul offered for our human plight before God posed a potential problem for his Jewish readers. For them, it was not Roman laws that were most important; it was their moral laws—the laws of Moses, like the Ten Commandments that were literally written in stone. Romans 3:19-20 succinctly exposes the problem the Jewish people faced.

   a. What is the law *not* able to do?

   b. But what valuable role does the law (for example, the Ten Commandments) play? How does that relate to the metaphor of a mirror?

2. Paul comes back to the issue of the law in Romans 7. Read verse 7.

   How does this show us that the law is like a mirror?

3. **In the rest of chapter 7 (verses 8-25) Paul describes a great struggle.**

    What was the source of Paul's struggle?

    Reflecting on your own life: How can you relate to that struggle?

4. **Mart De Haan ends this session by sharing his imagination of the emperor or governor going down to the arena floor and motioning aside a poor struggling gladiator or Christian, and then fighting for him and even voluntarily dying in the place of this poor struggling fighter.**

    Romans 5:8 says, "God demonstrates His own love toward us, in that while we were still sinners, Christ died for us" (NKJV).

    a. How does this verse summarize the good news that God does for us what we can't do for ourselves?

    b. How does this verse correlate with the scene Mart described?

5. **In Romans 8:28-39 Paul tells of the wonderful things God has done for us through Christ.**

    How does this passage further relate to the scene Mart described?

Reflecting on your own life: How does reading this passage make you feel? What is the proper response to what God has done for us?

DAYLIGHT ON PRAYER

A Time to Share

1. In light of the image of Christ fighting our battles, how do you need His power and strength right now?

2. What other people and needs are you concerned about?

3. Spend time together as a group praying for each other and your concerns.

DAYLIGHT AHEAD

Imagine standing in front of ruins that are nearly two thousand years old—seeing stones that were toppled that long ago and yet are still lying where they hit the ground. And imagine that the building was not just any edifice—it was the great temple of Jerusalem. Join Mart De Haan and Jimmy DeYoung as they reveal a close-up look at both the stones and at what the temple may have looked like so long ago. And join them as they explain what the destruction of that temple has to do with Paul's letter to the Romans.

A New Day Has Dawned

DAYLIGHT PREVIEW

A Visit To Jerusalem

About forty years after Jesus' death, burial, and resurrection in Jerusalem, another important event took place in that city. Just as Jesus had predicted, Roman soldiers swept into the Holy City and destroyed the magnificent temple that stood in the heart of the city. Today the stones of that temple still lie strewn below the Temple Mount as a silent witness to that event. And in Rome, the Arch of Titus, built 10 years after the destruction of the temple, still stands as a visual record of that event. These events can be seen today as symbolic of a new day that has begun in God's calendar.

COME TOGETHER

Icebreaker Questions

1. When you were growing up, how did you feel about sports games on the playground when two "captains" chose teams one kid at a time?

2. Have you ever visited the site of the ancient temple in Jerusalem? If so, what stood out to you the most?

3. What event caused you great sadness as a child?

FINDING DAYLIGHT

Experience the Video

Feel free to jot down notes as you watch the presentation by Jimmy DeYoung and Mart De Haan. Use the space below for those notes.

―――――――――――――**VIDEO NOTES** ――――――――

Jerusalem

Israel's temple

Paul's letter

Paul's turning point

God's plan

The Arch of Titus

What Israel lost

Grace, not race

God's unfolding plan

WALKING IN THE DAYLIGHT

Discussion Time

—————— UNDERSTAND THE CULTURE ——————

Background Questions

1. As we saw in the DVD, Israel had a magnificent temple in the time of Jesus. What do you think was the reaction of the Jewish people when their temple was destroyed in AD 70?

2. How do you think the Jewish people felt about the Arch of Titus that was erected in Rome ten years later?

DISCOVER GOD'S WORD
Discussion/Application Questions

1. Passages like Mark 13:1-2 show us that Jesus knew that the temple was going to be destroyed.

   How do you suppose Jesus' disciples felt when they heard Jesus' words?

2. The apostle Paul had a dramatic conversion. Read about his pre-Christian life (when he was known as Saul) in Acts 7:59–8:3 and Acts 9:1-2.

   How would you characterize Saul's attitude toward followers of Christ?

3. The rest of the story in Acts 9 recounts Saul's conversion. About twenty-two years later Paul wrote the letter to the Romans. Read Romans 9:1-5.

   a. How would you characterize Paul's attitude toward his fellow Jews who were *not* followers of Christ?

   b. Why did his feelings run so deep?

4. **In Romans 9:30-33 Paul compares Gentiles who followed Jesus with Jews who did not.**

   What is the "stumbling stone"? Why were the Jewish people stumbling over it?

DAYLIGHT ON PRAYER

A Time to Share

1. Do you have any personal requests you would like to share with the group?

2. Paul had great sorrow in his heart because of the unbelief of his fellow Jews. Are there individuals whose spiritual needs cause you to have deep sorrow?

3. In addition to praying for the situations and concerns that have been mentioned, pray together for the salvation of the Jewish people.

DAYLIGHT AHEAD

Mart De Haan and Jimmy DeYoung walk the busy streets of Jerusalem, reminding us that the people of that city and the land of Israel are still looking for Messiah to return. They discuss the anticipation the Jews still have for the future—including their plans for a rebuilt temple. Is there hope for Israel? Mart and Jimmy discuss that in our next session.

Messiah Hope

DAYLIGHT PREVIEW

Looking Forward

Did you know that in rooms not far from the Temple Mount in Jerusalem, Jewish craftsmen have constructed implements that they hope some day to carry into a newly built temple? Today, a mosque stands on the location of the temple that was destroyed in AD 70—and the anticipated location of a new temple that will house those implements. Yes, the Jewish people of Jerusalem are looking forward. But the apostle Paul also looked forward to what will be in store for the Jewish people some day. In Romans 11, you can read what he said about Jews and the future.

COME TOGETHER

Icebreaker Questions

1. Jimmy DeYoung says that he and his wife really enjoy sitting on Ben Yehuda Street in Jerusalem (where they live) and just watching the people go by. Where do you like to do that?

2. What special memory do you have of either giving or receiving flowers?

3. When you were growing up, did your family have any rules about things you couldn't do on the Sabbath or Sunday? Did you have any traditions about things you often would do?

 FINDING DAYLIGHT

Experience the Video

Feel free to jot down notes as you watch the presentation by Jimmy DeYoung and Mart De Haan. Use the space below for those notes.

─────── VIDEO NOTES ───────

Modern Jerusalem

Is God done with Israel?

Looking to the future

Jewish Christians

Temple preparation

Unfulfilled anticipation

Jews and Gentiles

Mart's personal message

 WALKING IN THE DAYLIGHT

Discussion Time

―――――――――― **UNDERSTAND THE CULTURE** ――――――――――
Background Question

We learn from the DVD that many preparations have already been made for a future temple to be built when the Messiah comes to Jerusalem. We also heard, specifically from Pastor Meno Kalisher, that although devout Jews today expect such amazing events to happen in the future, they are not open to the good news about Jesus the Messiah. Why is that?

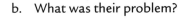
Discussion/Application Questions

1. **In Romans 10:1-4 Paul continues to write about his Jewish country-men in relation to the gospel.**

   a. What was Paul's hope and prayer for his fellow Jews?

   b. What was their problem?

   c. What was God's solution?

2. **In Romans 11:17-24 Paul writes about Jews (the natural, or original, branches) and Christian Gentiles (a wild olive shoot). Read verses 17-21.**

   What attitude should the Christian Gentiles have?

3. **Read Romans 11:22-24.**

   What hope remains for the Jews?

4. **Though Paul continues to address Christian Gentiles in Romans 11:25-36, he says some amazing things about the Jewish people.**

   a. What attitude does Paul exhort the Christian Gentiles to have?

   b. What do you think the "mystery" is that Paul was writing about?

   c. Though there are various interpretations about whom "all Israel" (verse 26) refers to, it is clear that God has not completely and permanently rejected the Jewish people (see also Romans 11:1). God has allowed a period of disobedience on the part of both Jews and Gentiles so He can have mercy on both groups. What confidence can we as Christians have as we pray for and witness to the Jewish people?

5. **Mart De Haan concludes this session by reflecting on Paul's analogy of the olive tree in light of Romans 10:13: "Everyone who calls on the name of the Lord will be saved."**

   Mart says, "The Messiah that has come—the seed, the descendant of Abraham—offers good news now, offers life and forgiveness and hope and security in relationship to God, to anyone who believes. It gets very personal. It's personal because I realize that if the offer had not been opened to the Gentiles I wouldn't have any confidence of forgiveness. I'd have no real hope of eternal life. I wouldn't have the benefits of a relationship with Israel's Messiah."

Reflecting on your own life: How "personal" does Paul's letter to the Romans get to you?

DAYLIGHT ON PRAYER

A Time to Share

1. Mart De Haan observes that the practice of Sabbath-keeping reminds devout followers of Judaism to stop, to rest, and to remember once every week that their survival and existence in the Promised Land is not the result of their own work or effort but is a gift from the loving heart of their Creator. How regularly do you stop to rest and to remember what God has done for you? Do you need to do more of that?

2. Do you have a specific need for rest or peace in your life today? In what other ways can the group support you in prayer today?

DAYLIGHT AHEAD

Do you remember hearing about the Jesus Movement of the 1960s? Jimmy DeYoung and Mart De Haan say there was a much earlier "Jesus Movement" in the first century. In this session, Jimmy and Mart visit the seat of Israel's government, the Knesset, to explain how government and religion sometimes have a tense relationship. They explore Paul's letter to the Romans and talk to a couple of pastors in Jerusalem to get a fresh perspective on how any "Jesus Movement" should interact with the government of the country where it is operating.

Church and State

DAYLIGHT PREVIEW

When Worlds Collide

What do we do when the church and the state conflict? We may think it's a fresh problem—that the problems twenty-first century believers have with an encroaching government are new. But the issue of a faith that seems to challenge the state is as old as the apostle Paul and his letter to the Romans. Paul challenged the status quo. How can his words be applied today? Perhaps that can best be seen by listening to two Jerusalem pastors who live under the law of today while seeking to honor the Word of God as written by Paul in Romans 13.

—— COME TOGETHER ——

Icebreaker Questions

1. This session begins with Jimmy DeYoung and Mart De Haan in front of the Knesset building in Jerusalem. What government building has particularly impressed you when you visited it?

2. Have you ever participated in a public demonstration of some sort?

3. What was your attitude toward authority when you were growing up?

4. Nizar Touma pastors an Arab church in Israel, where his people are both an ethnic and religious minority. In what way can you relate to being part of a minority?

FINDING DAYLIGHT

Experience the Video

Feel free to jot down notes as you watch the presentation by Jimmy DeYoung and Mart De Haan. Use the space below for those notes.

—————————————— VIDEO NOTES ——————————

A threat to the empire

The menorah and the Knesset

Paul's letter and the government

Meno Kalisher

Nizar Touma

Culture of love

WALKING IN THE DAYLIGHT

Discussion Time

──────────── UNDERSTAND THE CULTURE ────────────
Background Questions

1. How did Christianity, though committed to nonviolence and goodwill, challenge the authority of the Roman Empire, as it had first challenged the religious leaders of Israel?

2. What impressed you about the Jewish pastor, Meno Kalisher, and the Arab pastor, Nizar Touma, who spoke in this session?

DISCOVER GOD'S WORD

Discussion/Application Questions

1. Paul's letter to the Romans, which was addressed to the very center of the Roman Empire, includes some interesting implications about a Christian's relationship to government. Read Romans 13:1-5.

    a. What attitude are believers to have toward governing authorities?

    b. Paul says that the governing authorities have been established by God. In what situations is this sometimes hard to understand?

    c. Are there exceptions to the rule that we should obey the government? (See Acts 4:18-20 and Acts 5:29 if needed.)

2. Paul gets quite specific in Romans 13:6-7. Instructing the Christians at Rome about their attitude toward the governing authorities, he writes, "If you owe taxes, pay taxes; if revenue, then revenue; if respect, then respect; if honor, then honor" (v. 7).

    Which of those four are the most difficult for you to "pay"?

3. As we see in the next portion of Paul's letter, Romans 13:8-10, Paul expresses the principles of a culture of love.

What does Paul mean when he says that love is the fulfillment of the law?

DAYLIGHT ON PRAYER

A Time to Share

1. Read Romans 12:9-10 again. How can you follow these instructions more faithfully at home? At work? At church? In this group?

2. What prayer requests would you like to share with the group?

DAYLIGHT AHEAD

Pastors Meno Kalisher and Nizar Touma return to talk about the concept of transformed living—a concept Paul gave us in his letter that changed the world. What is the one element of Christianity that makes it stand out from both the Roman culture and from our culture today? Dr. Douglas Moo and pastors Meno Kalisher and Nizar Touma talk about that transforming element in our next session.

SESSION 10

Transformed Living

DAYLIGHT PREVIEW

Against the Tide

What do you do when you feel as if your faith makes you swim upstream in a culture that is swiftly going the other direction? The apostle Paul suggests that you make a sacrifice—a living sacrifice. In the first century, this new faith—Christianity—brought a new paradigm into the Roman culture. It taught that the individual is important and that God is personal. If the people were to make a difference in a culture and a government that ran counter to those truths, they would have to stop conforming to that world system and be transformed. That is still true. Two people who are dedicated to the truths of Paul's teaching are Meno Kalisher and Nizar Touma, pastors in Israel today. They help us see how Paul's teaching of not being conformed to this world can work in modern culture.

COME TOGETHER
Icebreaker Questions
---

1. Nizar Touma, pastor of an Arab congregation in Nazareth, says that his people need to stop making statements about "us" and "them." When you were growing up, who were the "us" and "them" groups?

2. Romans 12:2 tells us not to be "conformed to this world." How did peer pressure affect you the most as a teenager?

3. In what ways were you a nonconformist then? In what ways do you see yourself as a nonconformist now?

 FINDING DAYLIGHT

Experience the Video

Feel free to jot down notes as you watch the presentation by Jimmy DeYoung and Mart De Haan. Use the space below for those notes.

──────────────── **VIDEO NOTES** ────────────────

Renewal and the Roman world

Paul's strategy

A new kind of sacrifice

How does this work?

Meno

Nazir

Countercultural living

Two timeless truths

WALKING IN THE DAYLIGHT

Discussion Time

————————— UNDERSTAND THE CULTURE —————————

Background Questions

1. Gregory DiPippo states that Roman society was very much looking for renewal. Why was that true?

2. What does DiPippo mean when he says that the renewal Christianity brought was the notion of "person"?

3. The other reason DiPippo gives for Christianity bringing renewal to the Roman Empire was the idea that God came to the world and became one of us. How would that message spark renewal?

———————— DISCOVER GOD'S WORD ————————
Discussion/Application Questions

1. **In Romans 12, Paul focuses on the practical application of what he has previously written, calling for his readers to let Christ be Lord of every area of their lives.**

   What action does Paul call for in Romans 12:1?

2. **In Romans 12:2 Paul says, "Do not conform any longer to the pattern of this world."**

   What does that mean?

3. **Paul continues in this verse by telling the Christians at Rome to "be transformed by the renewing of your mind."**

   a. Jewish pastor Meno Kalisher says that to renew our minds means (1) to study the Word of God; (2) to pray in order to internalize and obey God's Word; and (3) to fellowship with other believers in order to be built up and encouraged.

Reflecting on your own life: How well are you doing in each of those three areas?

b. Arab pastor Nizar Touma speaks about our minds being renewed in the realm of our relationships. If we have the mind of Christ, we will have to forget who we are and stop focusing on "us" and "them." We will look at people through the eyes of Jesus. We will love them with the love of Jesus—even if we had formerly considered them enemies.

Reflecting on your own life: How well are you doing in these areas?

4. **Dr. Douglas Moo states that the New Testament "teaches a way of life that is always going to be countercultural. Human cultures tend to operate on the basis of selfishness, greed, power. And the Christian church is a place that is not to operate that way. It's supposed to be a place where love and peace and joy reign, where sacrificial love is to mark who we are as a people of God."**

How countercultural is the church today?

Reflecting on your own life: How countercultural is your life?

5. Mart De Haan concludes this session by saying, "When we think about the content of what Paul wrote in this letter, there are two mistakes we can make. We can either try to live the life of Christ without first experiencing a faith relationship with Him, or we can invite Him into our lives by faith and then miss the implications of walking with Him in our relationships with one another and with our neighbor and with the government."

   a. In what ways can you identify with either of these mistakes?

   b. In his letter to the Romans, Paul unfolds what it means to first have a relationship with God, and then he applies that relationship to everyday life. What are some practical ways we can apply our faith to the life we live in our culture?

DAYLIGHT ON PRAYER

A Time to Share

1. Gregory DiPippo points out that every person is the subject of God's love and mercy, and that God is so interested in our good that He came to the world and became one of us. How is that care and concern providing needed encouragement in your life right now?

2. Who else are you concerned about today? How can you pray together for their good?

DAYLIGHT AHEAD

Churches in Jerusalem? It might be a surprising place to start in a city noted mostly for its roots in the Jewish synagogue system. But that's where Jimmy DeYoung and Mart De Haan find themselves as they begin to explore the teaching of Paul the apostle about the church. They then move on to Caesarea as they examine how Paul's message helped the people see how Jews and Gentiles could be joined together in this new entity: the Christian church.

Paul's Peace Movement

The Church Begins

One man. One message. And it changed the world. The apostle Paul took the message of faith in Jesus Christ and transported the good news throughout the Mediterranean region—so much so that in Romans 15:19, he said, "From Jerusalem all the way around to Illyricum, I have fully proclaimed the gospel of Christ." The missionary journeys of Paul took a new peace movement—peace in Jesus Christ—to several nations, helping to establish churches that brought together Jews and Gentiles as never before had been done.

--- COME TOGETHER ---

Icebreaker Questions

1. Do you have any special memories of church bells ringing?

2. What is the most impressive church building you can remember visiting?

3. In this session Jimmy DeYoung and Mart De Haan visit the site of the great aqueduct in Caesarea. What engineering wonder stands out to you from your sightseeing experiences?

4. Who was the peacemaker in your family when you were growing up?

FINDING DAYLIGHT

Experience the Video

Feel free to jot down notes as you watch the presentation by Jimmy DeYoung and Mart De Haan. Use the space below for those notes.

———————————— VIDEO NOTES ————————————

Churches in Jerusalem

The beginnings of the church

The good news

Caesarea

Paul's transformation; Paul's mission

Paul's imprisonment

The sword of truth

Paul's message of unity

WALKING IN THE DAYLIGHT

Discussion Time

———————— UNDERSTAND THE CULTURE ————————
Background Questions

Gregory DiPippo states that the message of Christianity is that God has taken the fullness of our humanity unto himself and united it to the fullness of His divinity. That reality involves every single individual. And therefore there is no fundamental difference between a slave girl and the Roman emperor.

1. How do you think that message was received in the empire?

2. How does the good news that peace with God can be found through acceptance of the sacrifice of His Son challenge the class distinctions of society today?

——————— DISCOVER GOD'S WORD ———————
Discussion/Application Questions

1. **In this session Jimmy DeYoung speaks from the possible location of Paul's brief imprisonment in Jerusalem, which likely occurred just before Paul wrote Romans. At the time of his arrest, which was accompanied by an uproar against him, Paul received permission from the Roman commander to speak to the crowd. Read, in Acts 22:1-22, what Paul said.**

    Why did the crowd of Jews react so strongly to what Paul said in verse 21?

2. **Soon Paul was transferred to Caesarea, where he eventually appealed his case to Caesar. Paul appeared before King Herod Agrippa during that time, and again he recounted his conversion. Pick up the story by reading Acts 26:9-18.**

    What was Christ's commission to Paul in regard to both Jews and Gentiles?

3. **Paul continued his defense in Acts 26:19-23.**

    How did Paul respond to Christ's commission? What was the result?

4. In Romans 1:16 Paul wrote, "I am not ashamed of the gospel, because it is the power of God for the salvation of everyone who believes: first for the Jew, then for the Gentile."

In his letter to the Romans, how do we see Paul's calling and attitude, which is reflected in his statement here?

5. Later in his letter, Paul challenged his readers to implement the peace that they have with God in their relationships to each other. Read Romans 15:7-12.

   a. How was Jesus the model for their relationships with one another?

   b. How did He serve the Jews through His life on earth?

   c. What does this string of Old Testament quotations say about God's plan for the Gentiles all along?

6. How did Paul pray for the Romans in Romans 15:13?

DAYLIGHT ON PRAYER

A Time to Share

1. Romans 15:13 mentions at least five things that every person needs: hope, joy, peace, trust in God, and the power of the Holy Spirit. Do you feel as if you have any of those in abundance? Are any of them in short supply?

2. What prayer requests would you like to share with the group?

3. As you pray for each other, thank God for His gifts of hope, joy, and peace.

DAYLIGHT AHEAD

Imagine a time when there was no church as we know it—a time when there was no entity that united people of various backgrounds under one Lord. That's the kind of world in which Paul lived. Yet his message in the book of Romans changed all that. Come with Jimmy DeYoung and Mart De Haan as they visit some historic churches in Jerusalem and as they tell the unifying story of the first few centuries of the church.

SESSION 12

The Church United

DAYLIGHT PREVIEW

From Homes to Caves to Buildings

Church. Where you worship today is a far cry from the places where Christians worshiped in Paul's day. The people Paul wrote to were not united by a huge building where they met together. Instead, they met in homes or in caves. And in those locations, people who would not normally associate with each other would meet together in Jesus' name. Not until many years later would actual church buildings be constructed. Yet no matter where the people worshiped, early Christians began to demonstrate to their surrounding communities what it meant to live and work and worship together.

—————————— COME TOGETHER ——————————

Icebreaker Questions

1. What is the "coolest" cave you can remember visiting?

2. How do you feel about reciting the Lord's Prayer? Does that bring back any special memories?

3. Is there a story behind how you got your name?

FINDING DAYLIGHT

Experience the Video

Feel free to jot down notes as you watch the presentation by Jimmy DeYoung and Mart De Haan. Use the space below for those notes.

────────────────── **VIDEO NOTES** ──────────────────

The church in Paul's day

A new community

Paul's fate; continuing faith

The story of Constantine

Pater Noster

Paul's admonition: Unity

Diversity in chapter 16

Paul's ultimate message

What Paul wanted the people to know

WALKING IN THE DAYLIGHT

Discussion Time

────────── UNDERSTAND THE CULTURE ──────────
Background Questions

1. Three historic churches in or around Jerusalem are linked to the Roman Emperor Constantine, about three hundred years after Christ. What is so ironic about that?

2. One church in Jerusalem is referred to as Pater Noster. All around the entrance and the courtyard, the Lord's Prayer is written in over one hundred languages, beginning with "Our Father," or *"Pater Noster"* in Latin. Mart De Haan says that the apostle Paul would have loved this. Why?

DISCOVER GOD'S WORD

Discussion/Application Questions

1. **Mart De Haan points out that when Jesus talked about building His church, He wasn't talking about building with physical stones. He was talking about building people. And Paul's letter to the Romans was written to encourage believers to care for one another, even as Christ had cared for them.**

   In what way are church buildings an asset to churches today? In what way are they a liability?

   Reflecting on your life: What would happen if your church were forced to meet in homes rather than in a separate building?

2. **Beginning in Romans 14:1, Paul turns to some gray areas, or "disputable matters," in which the believers in Rome needed some help in regard to unity. Those who had "weak" faith were almost certainly Jewish Christians who had sensitivities regarding Jewish practices such as food restrictions and keeping the Sabbath. Those who had**

"strong" faith were the Gentile Christians—along with some Jewish Christians who believed that they were not bound to these obligations. Read Romans 14:1-4.

a. What attitude should the "strong" have toward the "weak"?

b. What attitude should the "weak" have toward the "strong"?

3. Paul continues this discussion in Romans 14:5-8.

How can both the one who eats meat and the one who abstains do so "to the Lord"?

4. In Romans 14:13-23 Paul tips his hand regarding his own position on these gray issues (see also Romans 15:1).

a. Did Paul see himself as a "weak" or "strong" Christian?

b. What would you see as a modern example of the type of gray areas that Paul was writing about? What would lead "to peace and to mutual edification" (Romans 14:19) in that situation?

5. In Romans 15:1-6 Paul again calls for members of the church to build each other up.

Does "a spirit of unity" (Romans 15:5) require agreement on all issues?

Reflecting on your own life: How hard is it for you to disagree in love with other believers?

6. Dr. Douglas Moo states that as God transforms individual human beings there is the potential to transform society as well. We see in Romans, with its emphasis on the community of Christ—the church, that "God wants us to learn to live together in a way that creates a new society—a counterculture—where *truly* peace and love and joy will reign."

Reflecting on your own life: What is the closest you have come to being part of a Christian community where peace and love and joy truly reigned?

Reflecting on your own life: How much do you long for that experience now?

7. As Paul concludes his letter, he expresses affection for many of the Christians in Rome by name and in the process tells us something about the diversity of the church. Dr. Douglas Moo notes, "Here we

have names of people who were slaves; people who had been freed from slavery; names that would have been given to aristocrats in Roman society at that time; names given to Jews; names given to Gentiles. In other words we sort of have a kind of a microcosm in Romans 16 of the Christian community as a place where people from all kinds of walks of life come together and are united."

Reflecting on your own life: How diverse is the constituency of your church? How do you feel about that reality?

DAYLIGHT ON PRAYER

A Time to Share

1. Mart De Haan concludes by observing that the message of simple faith in Christ, found in Romans, is "our hope, our salvation, our forgiveness, our assurance that we have a relationship with our Father." How assured, or confident, do you feel in your relationship with God?

2. What have you appreciated the most about this series and about this group? How can the group continue to support you in prayer?

3. Conclude your time of prayer by praying the Lord's Prayer together.

   "Our Father in heaven, hallowed be your name, your kingdom come, your will be done on earth as it is in heaven. Give us today our daily bread. Forgive us our debts, as we also have forgiven our debtors. And lead us not into temptation, but deliver us from the evil one."